MW00488053

RAISED
IN THE PEW

RAISED
IN THE PEW

RE'NA L. GARCIA

TATE PUBLISHING
AND ENTERPRISES, LLC

Published by Tate Publishing & Enterprises, LLC
127 E. Trade Center Terrace | Mustang, Oklahoma 73064 USA
1.888.361.9473 | www.tatepublishing.com

Tate Publishing is committed to excellence in the publishing industry. The company reflects the philosophy established by the founders, based on Psalm 68:11,
"The Lord gave the word and great was the company of those who published it."

Book design copyright © 2014 by Tate Publishing, LLC. All rights reserved.
Cover design by Rtor Maghuyop
Interior design by Jomar Ouano

Published in the United States of America

ISBN: 978-1-63185-539-9
Religion / Christian Ministry / Youth
14.07.11

For my fellow PK's, this book is truly dedicated to you.

"Speaking as a 4th generation preacher's kid (PK), I can say that growing up in a pastor's home is a unique experience. Funded by dozens of real-life stories, Re'na Garcia captures many of the privileges and challenges related to the life of a PK. In the end, Garcia offers multiple insights and suggestions to parents who are raising children in ministry settings. This is a insightful and helpful read for the entire pastoral family."

—Rev. Curtis Cole, Administrative Director,
Chi Alpha Campus Ministries, U.S.A.

Once in a while you read a book you wish you would have read forty years ago. For me this was one of those books! Written by a PK about PK's and their parents, it is a must-read for pastors and their spouses. One of the primary goals in our Ministry Network is to have healthy leaders. This book will be a great resource for us as it addresses the health of the pastors' home, which is foundational for an effective ministry.

Alan Warneke, Network Pastor/Superintendent

Raised in the Pew is a challenging, honest look at kids growing up with parents in pastoral vocations. The truth revealed here is that when parents say, "yes" to ministry, their entire family says "yes" together. Rena gets it, because she has lived it, both as a pastor's kid and now as a parent. Her own experience, insight, and love for both the kids and work of pastoral ministry, makes this book valuable for anyone desiring a raw look into how it impacts the entire ministry family.

George Stull, Community Care Pastor
HopePark Church, Nashville, TN

ACKNOWLEDGMENT

Thank you to my husband, Aaron, for believing in me and pushing me to complete this book. During the times I felt completely unqualified, you reminded me of God's calling. You are much more than a best friend to me, and I love you deeper every day.

CJ, Aly, and Parker, my beautiful kids. You are my inspiration. I pray for you daily that you will grow up loving being a PK. I pray you grow up always seeking Jesus and a deep committed relationship with him. You are the greatest joys of my life, and I love you with every ounce of my being.

My parents. As growing up a PK had some drawbacks, I could not be more grateful for you. I am so thankful that I can live out your legacy. You guys are the most selfless, giving, humble, compassionate people I've ever known. Dad, thank you for teaching me that compassion is inconvenient. Thank you for pounding into my head to find a need and fill it and to always be thinking outside of myself. Witnessing you both ministering to the entire community growing up has been invaluable to me. Not only having community ministries that feed, clothe, and keep hundreds of people warm through the year, but watching you minister when nobody was looking has made me the woman that I am today. I couldn't be more grateful for the influence you have on my family's lives! *You are my heroes!*

My sisters, Amy and Krista, thank you for making me think that I can do anything. Thank for being my best friends in the entire world, for loving me when I am unlovable, for teaching me with such grace. Thank you for believing in me, pushing me, and never letting me feel sorry for myself or give up. I can never put it into words what you've done for me. I cannot believe how lucky I am to have you as sisters. Krista, thank you for helping me to write the very best parts of this book.

George and Debbie, you will never know how much you imparted to Aaron and me over the years. Thank you so much for being amazing mentors. Thank you for holding us accountable and for teaching us how to be loving parents as well as pastors. I am forever grateful for the influence you have had in our lives.

For all of my friends, family, our bonus child Kimmy, my in-laws Jess and Judy, my Papa Bob and Cecy, my Church on the Move family, and my SONK family who encouraged me through this process, thank you. Your love and support means everything to me!

CONTENTS

INTRODUCTION

When God gave me the idea for this book eight years ago I immediately began taking surveys and interviewing every PK I knew. As I continued interviewing over the years I encountered numerous people that grew up with many of the same experiences that I had. The range of emotions that we all shared during interviews was so interesting. There are a definitely perks to being a PK. We often get the best parts in the plays, sing the special songs, you get special attention from church members. You are special, you need or get to be different because of who your parents are. You don't have to ask to use church stuff and pretty much get to roam free. Funny how most pastors kids are more than comfortable in the church, I can remember my dad telling me all the time, "This isn't your bedroom." In these interviews there were times where we laughed till it hurt, times where we cried, times where there was anger, times of regret, times of complete confusion. What I personally experienced more than anything was healing and restoration. This book was written to help you to understand what children who grow up in a ministry setting might encounter. The feelings and the stories that many of us share are included on the following pages. I don't claim to have all the answers or solutions, I simply write from personal experience and the experiences of over one hundred other pastors' kids. Pastor's Kids are set apart, for numerous reasons. Maybe you've never thought that being a Pastor's Kid is a job, but it really is. Experience has taught me this valuable lesson; from the time that you as a parent dive into the ministry your children join you. From that point on, for you and your family, your life is no longer your own.

As ministers we share our lives with people, we open our homes and lives to countless families. With parents in ministry children have no choice but to be involved. Whether your children serve at the church or not they are still affected by the fallout of the politics, staff changes, membership changes, your stress level, financial hardships, busy seasons, or your travel schedule. To gather information and stories for this book I have given a survey and spoken with over one hundred pastors' kids from all walks of life and all different denominations. We all found it incredible and most of the time just plain funny how much we shared in common with having pastors for parents. Some segments of this book may hit closer to home for you than others. If your children are young or old it is my prayer that these words will bring an awareness and possibly healing to your family. As a PK now raising my own children in ministry I find myself doing some of the things I swore I would never do. Finding that even after living as a PK I too struggle to find a healthy balance between pastoring and parenting. I am a PK with a heart for PK's who just wants to help other families experience the healing and restoration that I've received. It is my desire to help prevent the next generation of PK's from experiencing some of the more negative sides of being raised in ministry. Pastors are appointed by God to live out this amazing calling and I appreciate and can identify with everyone who has dedicated his or her life to ministry. I've lived both sides of the coin and can truly say being a PK or a parent raising a PK is a monumental challenge! May this book bring you to a fresh perspective of your life dedicated to a calling and what that requires of your children and family.

SAVE THE WORLD, LOSE YOUR KIDS

"The saying is trustworthy: If anyone aspires to the office of overseer, he desires a noble task. Therefore an overseer must be above reproach, the husband of one wife, sober-minded, self-controlled, respectable, hospitable, able to teach, not a drunkard, not violent but gentle, not quarrelsome, not a lover of money. He must manage his own household well, with all dignity keeping his children submissive, for if someone does not know how to manage his own household, how will he care for God's church?"

—1 Timothy 3:1-16 (ESV)

It's been a really hard month at church. One of our favorite board members passed away suddenly, we are in a huge financial crunch and struggling to pay salaries and bills at the church. Had a run in with a disgruntled member over something that was said from the platform and they are now leaving the church and taking five influential families with them. We've all experienced this at one point in our churches. Maybe different scenarios but all the same we've all had very hard times in our ministry. Experiences that have left us emotionally drained, tired and on our knees begging God to help us make it through. I can remember times where my father was visiting multiple people at the hospital, praying with families while their loved ones passed on, and counseling failing marriages all the while being concerned for church finances. The pressure can be hard to bear sometimes. Being a Pastor and walking in the calling that God has placed on your life can be one of the most emotionally challenging occupations on earth. Recently, I was reading stats about Pastors and I came across a few that were staggering.

- An estimated 1500 pastors leave the ministry each month due to moral failure, spiritual burnout or contention in their churches.

- Eighty percent of pastors and eighty-four percent of their spouses feel unqualified and discouraged in their role as pastors.

- Fifty percent of pastors are so discouraged that they would leave the ministry if they could, but have no other way of making a living.

I've sat with countless pastors over the years who have felt unimportant, insignificant and unappreciated. They feel burnt out not only because of the job, but because of the pressure they receive from their senior pastor, direct reports, leaders, and coworkers. This is a harsh reality in the church world that most people are unaware of. Is being a pastor horrible? Definitely not. Being in ministry has many rewards and not every pastor has such a rough time. However, we've all had to jump over what seemed like insurmountable obstacles from time to time. These hurdles are more than likely the cause of the breakdown in many pastor's homes. Think about a man or woman that has a regular or even high-stress job in the world. Most of them have an ability that we do not. Most of them are able to come home after a long, emotional day at work and have an evening with the family, a good night's rest and then they're back at it the next day. This is a luxury that Pastors need to try to achieve. Pastors struggle to disconnect with their church. Try and think of the last time you went home and did not get a phone call, email, or text about church business, whether it was good or bad. Pastors become emotionally connected to their churches so much so that it is nearly impossible to even enjoy a vacation without dealing with issues.

> The major problem with being unable to disengage with the church is we cannot fully connect with our children and families.

I'm certain that all pastors have experienced at one time or another the inability to mentally separate themselves from the day-to-day operations of the church. Can you imagine a mechanic coming home stressed about his "strategic plan" to fix every car in the city? Or a school teacher staying up all night worrying about her lesson being "deep enough," or if her classroom layout will draw new students. I may be wrong but I doubt that this happens very often.

When pastors take their work home with them just think of the emotional weight and stress that can be transferred to their spouse or children. Imagine, you come home with your wheels still spinning about the offering numbers, the next event, an upcoming sermon series, strategic planning meetings, a counseling session gone bad, etc. Suddenly, you find yourself in the same house and even in the same room with your kids but completely disconnected and unaware of your surroundings. Our homes should be a place of safety and encouragement that our families can excel in. A question I tend to ask myself is, "Is my home a place that promotes a healthy, balanced Godly life?" We can never forget that when we bring stress and negativity into our homes, especially in the name of Christian service, we are not cultivating our family for God's best. In fact, we are in danger of showing our families a gospel that cannot overcome things like stress and frustration. A common misconception is the thought that if we are simply in the same house as our family, then we are spending time with them. But the truth is, our undivided attention is what's required of us in order to properly disciple our spouse and children. A PK once wrote that she would wait to ask her father specific questions while he was reading and engaged in social media on his phone. She knew good and well that when he was reading Twitter she could get just about anything she wanted as long as it was a yes or no question. Having both parents minister together as a team makes this double the impact on the kids. A PK from California shared that his mother would make close to fifty visits a week to church members, teach Sunday school, and play the piano on the worship team. You can imagine being so involved with the church that it would be hard to fulfill the role of being not only a good parent but also being a good spouse.

> The truth is that the church doesn't just drain out of us the time we spend with our family but also the energy we have to give to them.

Finding the balance between pastoring and parenting is a huge challenge and is different for each family. There is no one formula that will work for everybody. What is most important is that Pastors need to constantly be looking and trying to find ways to achieve this balance. Some Pastors I've known over the years have been able to accomplish this to a degree. My challenge to you is to find what works for your family and stick to it no matter what!

> "Your children never forget the significance that you place on them as your sons and your daughters." (Rev. H.B. London)

Absence makes the heart wander

My husband and I are partners in ministry. We are both called into full-time ministry and both love to serve. In many of our ministry experiences we have both been required to wear a lot of hats. As pastor and his wife we are often expected to attend all services, arrive early, and are generally the last to leave. As a pastor's wife I find myself getting very busy with basic church duties like organizing events, planning meetings, preparing for services, graphics, videos, not to mention serving in other areas of church that are in need of volunteers.

When my son was little, before he could even speak an entire sentence, he hated going to church. I would literally turn the corner a few blocks away and he would start to cry. I would day after day and week after week drag him there crying and full of anxiety. I figured that the problem was the nursery. The people, the other kids, the same goldfish snack week after week. I remember the time I said to him, "I know how you feel, buddy; Mommy never liked going to church all the time either!" DING DING DING… A light bulb went off. Oh my goodness, I was doing exactly what my parents did to me. If I had a quarter for every time I missed a church service, I would have about, hmmm… a quarter. I realized two things that day:

1. I was having my kids at church way too often. This is something I did not like growing up and here I was doing it to my own kids.

2. My son did not just dislike church, but he didn't like who "I" was at church. I was so busy dragging him around as quickly as possible tying up all the loose ends, stopping to talk to every person but not having enough time to run him to the bathroom, I was holding other people's babies and engaging their kids, running copies, setting up power point, all the while pulling my boy around the room by his arm, frustrated with him for fussing and slowing me down.

I did not even realize that it was actually me, not the nursery, that was giving him so much anxiety. No wonder he dreaded it there. I think back to those days and although I can't take them back, I wish I could. It would not have hurt anybody if I just walked by without stopping to share life stories while my son needed the rest room. Getting angry and frustrated with him when all I am doing is a thousand menial tasks just to make the church people see a seamless service, all seems so very unimportant on the grand scale. I gave my son the idea that church could turn me into a monster. I was too busy filling everybody else's needs to recognize the need of my own child. I don't know about you, but I want my kids to enjoy church, to love learning about Jesus, and I never want them to resent the church, God or me for that matter.

When I finally realized what was happening I began to lay a few things down so that I could give my kids a healthier view of the church. I needed to stop the pattern while he was still little. When I began to let go of some of my responsibilities at the church I actually went through a bit of a slump. I felt like God wasn't using me, like I wasn't doing enough. The Lord spoke to me, and very clearly said, "Your kids are your ministry."

I was pretty upset with myself that I had been missing it all along. We can have all the healthy ministries in the world, but how can we run a church properly if we can't even help to run your own household?

> What is the use in saving the lost if we ultimately lose our children?

I recently spoke with a PK in Oregon who is currently not serving the Lord and is quite bitter toward the church. She said that she has fine memories of growing up but both of her parents were so involved in the church she says she was left alone a lot and also she was responsible for keeping her siblings most of the time. She wished that her parents knew how to say no. Not to her, but to other people. Here are the words that she said ring in her head today, "Sorry I can't come to your game. We have worship practice." "Can you get a ride home? We had an emergency counseling session today." Can you put dinner on? Our prayer meeting ran a little long today." Now don't get me wrong, it's not wrong to ask your kids pitch in around the house. But when they begin to feel like they have to pick up too much slack because of your involvement in the church we need to recognize it and nip it in the bud. It is so important for us to keep our priorities straight.

1. Personally we must have a relationship with God.

2. You are married and must have a healthy relationship with your spouse.

3. You are a parent so you have a responsibility to have a relationship with your children.

4. You are a pastor and you have a responsibility to your church.

We must be sure that our family always comes before the church. It is important to display these priorities to our congregations. Some churchgoers may not like being all the way down at number 4 on your priority list. The people that have a problem being so far down on your list are the people that are unhealthy to be around your church and family. When they decide to leave your church you should not put up a fight; in fact you could help them make their exit strategy.

> Pastors and Pastor's wives can get so wrapped up in the needs of the people that we often miss the needs of our kids.

In almost every survey that I took, I found that so many PK's resented their parents for not being a bigger part of their lives. A PK from Kansas City shared this with me, "If my dad has time to go to the hospital, (and there is always someone in the hospital) then he should be able to find the time to come to my band concerts and basketball games." This statement made me chuckle because it was shared with me so many times. Another PK recalls her father coming to her volleyball game when she made the varsity team. She was nervous because it was her father's first time watching one of her games. She was waiting for a set and ready to slam it down, super excited to make her father proud. Just before her big moment she looked over to see him on his cell phone, probably talking to a board member or parishioner ironing out a totally unimportant detail. You won't be surprised to hear how this story ends; the only slam that happened that day was when she totally missed the spike and the ball slammed her in the face. Her father sat through her whole game, unfortunately that was the only part she could remember.

A 33-year-old PK Joan shared with me that if her father would just love her as much as he loved "John Smith," that maybe she would be a Christian now. She knows what is right and wrong and actually lives a very successful life, but has no desire to serve God or take her family to any church. It is incredibly sad that Joan is so bitter about the lack of her father's love in her life that she is now raising her own family and will have nothing to do with God. The saddest part is that when I asked this Joan, "Do you think that it is too late to restore your relationship with your father?" Her response was, "NO!" She still desperately seeks his love and approval. When I asked her what she felt would work for her, her answer was simple. Joan said, "All he has to do is call me. Be interested in my life and my kid's lives. I see them once a year but don't even talk to them other wise."

So, dads or moms, if you are reading this right now and you have a strained relationship with your daughters or sons, you may not even be aware of how they feel about you. Let me challenge you to do something right now. Put a bookmark in this book and call your kids right now. Tell them you love them, tell them that they are a gift from God, and ask them about their kids if they have them. How was their day or latest event? Make a small effort. This may be all it takes to get the ball rolling to restore a relationship that is vital to both of your lives. In the surveys and interviews that I did most of the PKs shared with me that their mothers played both roles in their lives, Mother and Father. It was a general consensus that their dads were around but not always present. A pastor wife friend of mine told me a story that just broke my heart. She shared with me that her son prayed in bed one night to get hurt real bad so his daddy would come be with him in the hospital. The bummer about this story is that the father actually thought that his kids were very content with their relationship. I could literally write stories all day about PK's feeling unloved, unappreciated, uncared for and ignored. Over and over again I have asked grown PK's what they will do differently as a parent. The number one answer was, "I will spend more time with my kids." Strangely, feeling unimportant breeds insecurities in kids that are very hard to reverse later in life.

In First Timothy, the Apostle Paul gives us a strong mandate for any father, especially one seeking spiritual leadership.

> "He must manage his own household well, with all dignity keeping his children submissive, for if someone does not know how to manage his own household, how will he care for God's church?"
>
> 1 Timothy 3:4,5 (ESV)

It is absolutely vital for fathers to be the priest of their home. It is completely possible to run a successful church and run a healthy household. I have sat in numerous church services and heard pastors preach wonderful convicting messages about raising healthy families and being parents. But as pastors we need to not only teach our church but also follow the plan we lay out for our churches. Lead them by example, show them how important your wife and children are to you. A PK from Tennessee wrote, "Pay attention to your kids at the right time and you won't have to pay attention at all the wrong times!"

HELPFUL HINTS:

1. At least once a week, plan a night that is dedicated to your wife and kids. Make a penalty for yourselves if you miss the family night. (Let your kids choose the penalty.) Shut off your phone and lock your door, make this fun so they know you're dedicating this time to them alone. No emails, social media or daydreaming about growing your church, etc.

2. Make an effort to be more involved in their school programs and sports. Be there for as many concerts as possible. Make your presence known at the events. Nothing is worse than when your parents show up at an event texting, talking on the phone, and totally distracted by something else.

3. A PK from Colorado mentioned to me that they were not allowed to skip church at all, not for any reason. She says, let your kids stay home from church when they are sick. I wasn't surprised at the amount of PK's that go to church sick. Dad has to be there, Mom has to be there, so you just have to buck up and go. I've heard stories of PK's sleeping in Dad's office, under chairs or pews, or in an office during church because they were sick and had no choice. The reason this is so paramount in a kid's life is because this just proves to your children that they take a backseat to the church.

If your kids are sick or just plain tired, it will not kill them to miss a church service. Make going to church partly their decision and I promise they will choose going to church more often than not.

4. When you are talking to your kids, make it a point to not answer your phone until the conversation is over. Turn the ringer off and tell your kids you want to hear about their day, or let them ask you questions. Let them see you ignore a call and focus on them; they will always notice when they have your attention.

5. Be sure and acknowledge them at church. Ask them questions about their teachers, peers, and the lessons that they are learning. Be very interested in the memory verses and handouts sent home.

6. A pastor friend we have worked with showed us a great tip for spending special time with our kids. He takes each of his kids out on the day of the month that corresponds with their birthday, so if their birthday is March 3rd, he takes that kid out on the 3rd of every month. It is a great way to remember to keep your calendar clear for those days.

7. Have family dinner at the table at least three times a week. When I say family dinner I don't mean everyone sits down to eat together and watch TV or play on their phones. I mean, no phones, no TV, no distractions, just

family engaging each other in conversation. In our house, we like to play games at the table, "Would you rather" or "Do you know me" are some great examples. "Would you rather" is a silly game that creates fun conversation with your family. You can find examples online. "Do you know me" is a game we made up in order to keep up with our children's lives as they are constantly changing while growing older. We simply go around the table and try to guess favorite colors, games, music, celebrities, etc. It keeps conversation light and fun and keeps me up to date.

REFLECTION:

1. Take a minute and write down a list of your current priorities in the context of church and family. Ask your kids to take a minute and write down what they think your priorities are.

2. Fathers, are you the priests of your home? Or does your wife have to cover that role because of your constant absence?

3. What would your wife answer if she was asked these same questions about you?

4. Write down some activities that you plan to do this month with your children.

TO PROTECT AND SERVE

Growing up as a PK helped me to develop all the talents I had and even some I didn't know I was blessed with! What other kid can say that they were part of the choir, the dance team, the stage crew, the A/V team, and still played the lead role in the Christmas production every year for twelve years? PKs can start their acting careers from birth as baby Jesus and graduate to Mary or Joseph by age thirteen. I guarantee you that a large percentage of PKs, male or female, knows how to make a beard out of coffee grounds or has used a Burger King crown for the all-important role of a wise man.

PKs play many different roles in their lives; some of these roles like, actor, singer, director, Sunday school teacher or secretary were given to them. Some they inherently give themselves, like brother, sister, counselor and friend. However, there is one role that is assumed by PKs that can be quite troublesome at times. It is one that is engrained into most PKs without anybody even knowing. This is the role of protector.

In my own life and interaction with countless PKs, I've found that a common thread amongst them is the overwhelming need to protect their parents. It's obviously very natural for kids to be protective of their parents. However, most children don't go to work with their parents and witness things like bad attitudes, eye rolling, brown nosing, business meetings gone bad, etc. As PKs we spend a better part of our lives at our parent's work place, the church, not only spending time with the church staff, but also a plethora of people who usually want some of your time or attention. Being involved in the church allows PKs to experience some wonderful parts of ministry. It also allows for your kids to see a potentially ugly behind the scenes atmosphere of the church. PKs from all over have shared with me about times of overhearing disgruntled churchgoers or staff members complaining about issues ranging from this week's sermon to a staffing decision that was made in a recent leadership meeting.

This feeling of protection is not just standing up for you with other people but also keeping quiet about things that may go on in your home. I believe that there is an unspoken rule that most every PK lives by. PKs will go to great lengths to keep our parents' integrity in tact. It's important that people see you in a good light. Constantly defending or keeping real-life situations quiet can be quite a burden for a kid. Your kids see all your fights, your flaws, your sins, and your weaknesses. They see what the average church attender will never see. I've heard countless pastors say phrases to their congregations like,

"I'm going to be real with you here for a minute" or "What you see, is what you get," or my very least favorite pastoral zinger, "I'm going to be transparent here for a minute." But let's be honest, you can't really be transparent with your congregation. Can you imagine getting up in front of your church and telling them that you are sick and tired of dealing with the whining and complaining that they need to just grow up. How about getting up in front of your congregation week after week and telling them about arguments you've had with your wife?

The bottom line is that your congregation does not really know all of you. They know about you, what you like, your favorite football team, some of them are even your closest friends. But let's get "real" for a minute; your family/kids are the only people who know every detail about you. They see the human side of you, the anger, fears, all the things that annoy you, and yet it is almost unbearable to hear or see anybody be negative towards you. Even if they don't agree with you or are in a stage of their life where they may not seem to like you at all, they would still do anything to keep your pastoral image and calling at the forefront of others. PKs are careful to keep you at a higher level for your church to see.

One of the biggest problems with your kids feeling the need to protect you is that when they are going through very difficult times, especially when you are involved, who can they talk to? PKs can't just confide in anyone. Several PKs shared in the fact that growing up they didn't have a lot of people to share their feelings with while facing difficult circumstances.

Don't get me wrong there are always a handful of people around offering a listening ear like, "Brother Tommy-Tell-All or Sister Sally-Shares-a-Lot." I know I would not dare share my frustrations with my life with just anyone in the church. Although "Sally-Shares-a-Lot" would sure get a kick out of hearing how my parents got into a huge fight last night.

Do people tell PKs that they can't share their problems with churchgoers? No. It really becomes a built-in defense mechanism that develops over the years. I've spoken with PKs who hid the fact that their parents abused them physically, down to a PK feeling like he needed to skirt around the fact that his dad watched a rated R movie. In most cases, nobody ever said don't tell, PKs just don't. Something inside of a PK just needs to keep their parents' reputations in high regard. I think that there is just a basic understanding that a lot of church members view their pastors as perfect and even sometimes like a super hero. Who do they call when they're in trouble, hurt, in the hospital, or facing serious family problems? They call you. Who comes to the rescue? You. Your children go to great lengths to protect you because they know how much people count on you. Sometimes, protecting our parents can be mistaken for keeping secrets or even lying. Please understand, I would never endorse a child keeping secrets or lying about important issues, but it is important that we help them find the "right" people to talk to if the need arises. Every kid needs someone they can trust to be able to share these things with. They need to be able to get counsel from someone other than you. If your child does not have a safe place to go or a safe person to talk to, they will find safety in a place or person that could be damaging to them later. Finding refuge in a person that we as parents don't approve of or a person that gives them guidance in the wrong direction happens more often than not. Finding a designated person that is a confidant for your child is key in raising a healthy kid. It's not about hiding your life and presenting a false family to the church, it's about keeping your family life somewhat separate from the church.

PKs also take great offense when somebody hurts you. They can hear so many things and see so much more than you probably realize. It is such a shame how often people feel the need to share their ill feelings towards you in front of your children. There are always going to be unhappy churchgoers in your congregation who feel it is their duty to tell you or any captive audience that they don't like the songs you've been choosing, the clothes you've been wearing, or my personal favorite, your current sermon series is not "deep enough." I still encounter these people from time to time who feel like if they drop a hint or two about a grievance they have with my father maybe it will get back to him. As a grown woman I politely hear them out and try my best to shake it off. Your children are exposed to these opinions of others more often than you may think. Unfortunately, the feeling of wanting to protect you, your image, and all you do just never go away. Your kids see how hard you work, they see the tears you cry, the love you pour out and the burdens you carry. When people speak negatively about you or even leave the church it can be just as hurtful to your kids as it is to you.

When I was sixteen years old I overheard a woman speaking negatively about my father. What she was saying was so silly and completely off base. In fact, it didn't bother my dad at all when he heard what she was saying. Eventually she left the church and it was for the best. Consequently, it took me years to forgive this woman. I didn't even know I was holding a grudge until years later when I ran into her at a birthday party. I left the party sick to my stomach until I realized the Lord was brining it to my attention that I had been hanging on to this offense for many years. I've since forgiven her, but for some reason I held onto those feelings for years. Instead of doing what my father did and just forgave and moved on, I just couldn't let it go. Unfortunately most PKs carry a lot of displaced anger towards church people.

A year ago, a PK from Oregon who's been out of the church life for twenty years shared with me that she still rarely goes to church because "church people are the worst." She went on to say, "They are all selfish, backstabbing, people." Twenty years later she goes to church only on Easter.

Jenny, a twenty-year-old PK from Nashville, was telling me that her father had just been asked to resign from their church of sixteen years. She is grown and in college now, but says that this is one of the hardest things that she has ever gone through. It literally pained her to see her parents hurt by the people they loved most, their church family. Not only that but she felt as if her life had suddenly turned upside down. She was suddenly and without reason separated from some of the relationships she held so dear. For sixteen years she was raised with an extended family of brothers, sisters, aunts and uncles. These family members are some of the very people that she felt had "turned" on her parents and caused the resignation. She was aware of the swirling rumors and horrible backstabbing and it broke her heart. She recalled people who felt like family, that had a huge part in her life just walk away and never spoke to her again. As with many pastor's kids, her parent's desire for acceptance was transferred to and absorbed by her. She was taught and encouraged by her parents to think of her church family as her real family. This created for a time a cocoon of false intimacy and a sense of security that never really existed. She learned that love is conditional, that there is an expiration date on relationships in the church.

When it comes to our children and their relationship with the church, they need to know that these relationships are a part in their walk with God. However, unlike your real family, whose love is unconditional, sometimes the parishioners act out of malice or insecurity, and it can be directed at them. We cannot expect people to love our children like we do. Pastor's kids agree that the church is made up of many kind, compassionate, loving people, all with an opinion. Many can recollect a special relationship with a church member that really meant a lot to them and even relationships with people who mentored them and helped them navigate through really tough situations. Explaining to your kids how relationships with church "family" members should look in advance will help cultivate the healthiest situation possible.

Good Intentions, Gone Wrong

As PK's carefully work to preserve the church's view of you, many PK's chimed in that the favor isn't always returned. Every pastor is looking for a really great story to share from the pulpit. A story that will have the congregation on the edge of their seats, a story that won't leave a dry eye in the building, whether it's funny or sad. Pastors read hundreds of books, blogs, emails, and magazines to seek out that incredibly heart-warming story to bring home a really great sermon. So let me ask you this, how many times in a sermon have you you used your children's mistakes or life lessons? How many times have you you told your congregation, in great detail, a mistake your kid has made? How many times in a counseling session or conversation with a church member have you brought up your PKs "life lessons"? Big or small, there needs to be boundaries on sharing. The truth about using our kids as examples is that is breaks the fabric of trust and security in our home.

A PK named Janet, who really has an amazing testimony that could change countless lives, once told me about how she tried to commit suicide when she was sixteen. She hesitated to share her story with me, it was very brief but incredibly effective. I won't tell you the details of her testimony because that would completely ruin my point. As she finished her story she thanked me for listening and asked if we could never speak of it again. I was taken back by her request. You see, she overheard her father in several counseling sessions share her story with people. He never meant to make her look bad or speak negatively of her; in fact he intended to do the opposite, to share her story to help others. Unfortunately for Janet, it just brought her extreme embarrassment, and judgment from church people. In fact she didn't even want to look certain church members in the eyes for a long time, because she was ashamed of her actions and now worried about being the topic of conversations. There was an instance of a well-meaning woman who approached Janet after a counseling session with her dad who offered to pray with Janet and be a listening ear because her child had recently gone through the same sort of situation. Janet was mortified that this woman knew she had tried to commit suicide. So early into Janet's recovery this was very damaging. She began to feel embarrassed and worthless every time it came up. What could have been a triumph and healing in her family continued to make Janet struggle with the same feelings that caused her to attempt suicide in the first place. Expounding on your PKs mistakes and life choices only serves to alienate them, to prove to them that their valued less than, not even equal to the people that sit in your pews. Janet is one of many examples of a PK that went to extreme lengths to protect her parents but felt like the, the protection was never reciprocated.

Pastors, we have to protect our children. I once had a woman, let's call her, "Sally," come up to me and tell me that she wished her Pastor, John, would just be real with the congregation. You see Sally's kid was a close friend with Pastor John's son. Because of their friendship Sally was aware of and even a part of the issues in this PKs life. Sally and the friends she had be talking too, (bless her heart) were upset with the pastor for not telling the congregation of his personal struggles with regard to raising *his* teenager. She rambled on and on about the need to be honest and upfront with the congregation. As a pastor's kid, I definitely had a different and less popular view of the situation. I looked at that woman and said, "Sally, that is a great point, thank you. I would like to offer you the first opportunity to share with all of the congregation from the platform, that your child has been going out and drinking on the weekends, or share with the church an argument that you had with your spouse?" Sally declined both of my offers, I just hope she did not decline to get my point. Should you embarrass your child by openly sharing her struggles with hundreds of people or should you work it out as a family and deal with it in private?

Your PK only has you to shield them, As parents and pastors we can allow them the grace to hurt and to heal privately.

You may need to protect your kids from the people who really just want to get the dirt on your family. People who just want to see your failures more than they want you to be real. There will most likely always be some of those in your congregation. Pastors, being real is imperative when leading people. Church people need to know that you're not perfect and that you make mistakes, humanity is an important quality in a pastor. Understand that your children are going to make mistakes and will make some really horrible decisions at times. Talk about it with them. Go ahead, laugh, hug, cry, yell but please, I beg you, protect them. Protect them from a body of people, a culture that inadvertently makes them feel the need to be perfect. Getting back to Janet, it would have been a great idea for her father, in advance to ask how she felt about him sharing her story. In this particular instance her fathers' sharing was very damaging even years later. Completely unintentional, heart-warming, emotion-gripping stories can often really hurt your kids.

HELPFUL HINTS:

1. Give your kids a designated, "Hold nothing back," "Tell all" person to talk to. Sit down in advance with this person and let them know that you've chosen them to be the one person that their kids can confide in. For our kids it's their Aunties. My sisters have my kids best interest in mind, want them to be good

people, make good decisions and be happy, well-adjusted, Jesus-following adults. For you it might be a grandpa, grandma, close friend, Godparents etc. Let your children know that they don't have to hide anything but you would like for them to not confide in just anybody. Let them know that you have mentors and friends that you share with as well. Not everyone needs to know all of the family business.

2. Ask your kids if you can share stories about them. Be specific about the story first and let them decide! A PK once told me that he collected $5 for every embarrassing story so he would often try to encourage his father to insert his embarrassing moments into his sermons. Go out of your way to protect them.

3. Give your teenagers an opportunity to share their testimony with you without fear of judgment, or punishment. Ask for permission to share in counseling sessions. Overhearing or being approached by someone who has heard the intimate details of your pitfalls from your father is far more damaging than being upfront and asking permission. If your teenager or grown kids are uncomfortable with this it's not skin off your teeth, right. There are millions of great stories out there to use in order to help a person in need.

REFLECTION:

1. Who is a person that you can trust for your kids to have honest conversations with? _____

2. Talk with your kids in advance and ask them who they would like this to be. Name 3 people that they can choose from.

3. Do you have set of ground rules with your kids and this person to talk about what is acceptable and appropriate to talk about?

4. Ask your children (if they are old enough) to share their testimony with you.

THE FISH BOWL

As a PK I have heard approximately 1 million parallels between objects, events, and foods to life. My father over the years has compared different situations in life to a Monopoly game, candles hiding from lighting up the dark and my personal favorite building the perfect taco. After hearing several PKs refer to their lives as living in a fishbowl, I began to study goldfish and their habitats. I found a few parallels that were definitely worth sharing.

Stunted Growth

A goldfish can grow up to two feet long and weigh up to nine pounds. Unfortunately for the goldfish it can only grow as big as its habitat. If you put your goldfish into a pond it would grow bigger and also live longer. It's the same with your kids. It is perfectly normal to want to place our kids in a fish bowl; I have to admit I find it desirable most days. After all it does protect from all the harmful, bacteria-laden, sharp-sided, hard-surfaced objects that this world has to offer. As parents we all want to keep our kids as safe as possible, because in our minds safety = happy, right? I've seen all different levels of parents attempting to shelter their children from this world. The following is a collection of examples PK's have given about their parents' restrictions on them.

1. "I was never allowed to attend public school."

2. "I was not allowed to have friends outside of the church."

3. "My parents wouldn't let me listen to secular music. They wouldn't even let me listen to Christian music if it didn't sound Christian enough."

4. "We had a piece of paper taped on our Dirt Devil vacuum that said Dirt Angel."

5. "We couldn't say, Deviled Eggs we said Angel Eggs."

6. "We were not allowed to watch any shows that had any sort of magic in them."

7. "We could not attend school events."

8. "Our family couldn't play sports in the summer because it might interfere with church camp."

9. "I was never allowed to go to a dance, or do any kind of dancing."

10. "I could not do any activities on Saturday nights because it might interfere with my dad's prep for Sunday mornings."

11. "Could never use the word, 'Lucky' we used the word, blessed."

12. "I was never allowed to participate in Halloween in any way shape or form. If a Halloween art project was going on at school I had to opt out."

13. "I was never allowed to make very many decisions, my parents chose the clothes I wore, the friends I hung out with, how I spoke, and had a tight rein on me all of my life. I was never given an opportunity to make many choices."

Shielding our kids from all things unholy can later lead to destruction. Nine out of ten PK's that I have interviewed have been through a wild phase at one time in their life. A lot of times leaving the home and entering the real world can be a shock and lead to major exploration of things they've never experienced. I hate to bring up Katy Perry, the token PK gone wild but reading an article about her the other day and her life growing up a PK she said it so well. "When I started out in my gospel music my perspective then was a bit enclosed and very strict, and everything I had in my life at that time was very church-related. I didn't know there was another world that existed beyond that. So when I left home and saw all of that, it was like, 'Omigosh, I fell down the rabbit hole and there's this whole Alice in Wonderland right there!'" — Perry in *The Scotsman*, 2009

> *John 17:14-18 says,*
>
> "I have given them Your word; and the world has hated them because they are not of the world, just as I am not of the world. 15 I do not pray that You should take them out of the world, but that You should keep them from the evil one. 16 They are not of the world, just as I am not of the world. 17 Sanctify them by Your truth. Your word is truth. 18 As You send Me into the world, I also have sent them into the world.

In this verse Jesus is praying for His disciples. Jesus understands the pressures of this world but he also understands the importance of being in it. Allowing our kids to be in the world but not a part of it can be tricky but this an imperative part of being a Jesus follower. God is constantly at work in the world. How can our kids fully grasp His greatness and power if they are unable see Him at work? Jesus didn't participate in sin but he also refused to isolate himself from sinners.

Sometimes we are forced as pastors to face the stark reality of people's expectations. No one wants to have a pastor that does not measure up to their version of holiness; our kids are also included in that measurement. So as dutiful pastors and people of the cloth they place their kids in the infamous Christian fish bowl. The goal of the parents should be to release a healthy, God-following adult or leader. How will your children learn to lead if they aren't exposed to experiences that require decisions, strength, and flexibility.

> Kids need guidance during trials rather than a lack of trials.

We need to be sure that our kids are safe but not unable to adapt to different situations.

Please don't tap on the glass

Being trapped in the fish bowl can be hazardous to your kids because there are people always watching and tapping the glass. We like to think that the tapping on the glass is very similar to all the remarks from the churchgoers. These comments can be an unhealthy bacteria that can have the opportunity to grow and pollute the tank, causing sickness and disease that in time will hurt your children. Bacteria forms and objects fall into the tank on a daily basis, but I've never seen a fish throwing it's waste or junk out of a tank. As a PK many things can leak in…criticism, harsh words, pressure and responsibility. A PK from Oregon told me a story about an elder that was close with her father who use to correct her on the way she dressed. One day she was wearing a t-shirt that said, "My foot is on the Rock, my name is on the Roll." It had a scripture about having your name in the book of life. This particular elder told her how inappropriate her shirt was because all you could read from far away was ROCK and ROLL. She quietly went home to change so she wouldn't be disrespectful. Seems so silly now, but when I asked if she ever told her parents of how people commented on her clothing she told me no. She didn't want to bother her parents with something like that, especially on a Sunday.

I personally was the recipient of numerous verbal corrections from church members in my life time. Our kids need to know that people can share their opinions with them and that they need to be respectful but you are the ultimate decision maker. If you approve the outfit, hair, makeup, attitude, language, then it is okay. It's important that you help your children learn how to dismiss criticism. Multiple PKs feel like it's not important to tell their parents about the judgments they face growing up. In the end it's these judgments, pressures, and harsh comments that form some of the unhealthy habits and personality traits that your children develop over time.

No place to hide

Another aspect of living in the fish bowl is that PK's feel like they are always being watched. From the inside, things that don't seem like a big deal are magnified by the people looking in.

Goldfish can be seen all the time from every angle; they can hide in little fake houses or plastic plants but that's just a light camoflauge, really you can see them all of the time. Many churchgoers seem to keep a close eye on the Pastor's kids behavior, attitude, how they speak, what they wear the list is endless and so is the pressure. A fifty-two-year-old PK wrote, "I hated the pressure of trying to be perfect, I got tired of everyone thinking I was, or needed to be a Bible scholar." Being watched and expected to perform does not just come from church people but also from us as parents.

A thirty-one-year-old PK once said she hated being drug to people's houses for dinner because they had to act like a perfect family. This PK was put off by this because her family had a lot of issues at home. She shared that most of the time right up until they entered peoples homes or the church her parents were fighting. She grew up learning how to put a smile on and fake it. As her story unfolded it was strikingly similar to so many other PKs. Being taught to live one way at home and another way in front of people instilled into this particular PK that it is ok to be a liar, fake, and insincere. As pastors we are drilling into our children the importance of being honest, yet sometimes the expectation we put on them is to in essence change their behavior based upon the people that they are around. It was sad for me to hear this woman share her experiences, she has a family of her own now and does not attend church or have a relationship with God. Sadly she feels today that all Christians are hypocrites, and the worst of them all are pastors.

This PK was not alone in feeling like she was shown her whole life how to put a smile on and pretend like everything was perfect. Another pastor's kid shared that he felt like all the rules and regulations placed on him were not to protect him or love him but for a different purpose. He felt like his parents purpose in "protecting" him was actually just to be able to present a pristine, innocent and holy child to a church body. It is this pressure that leaves most PK's feeling inadequate and unable to measure up. You have to ask yourself, am I the one hindering my child? Is putting all of these demands and expectations on them healthy? Could it be my fault that they are not becoming the person that God has called them to be? Will my own ideas and worries of how people feel about my kids, family, and parenting affect their relationship with the Lord in the long run? It is so important that we make every effort to let our kids grow up in a healthy environment. To let them fail when needed and teach them that they never have to try to be perfect.

HELPFUL HINTS:

1. You have to decide what is right for your children as far as how much of the world they can be involved in. I believe this only comes through constant prayer. As I

battled feelings of keeping my own children trapped in a fish bowl my mother gave me a wonderful thought that I now live by. "Don't focus on the what-if's, focus on the Hope." I was so engrossed in scenarios of what would happen to my children if exposed to the world too much that I believe I was hindering their growth. Not allowing our children to be exposed to non-Christian ideas can keep them from being prepared to enter adulthood. Praying constantly for our children and family helps to really focus on the Hope that we have in Jesus.

2. Always communicate with your kids about people's words. Ask them if church members are commenting to them about their behavior, attitude, or appearance. Teach your children that we will always receive criticism from people but we cannot let it dictate our lives. Show them how to let it roll off their backs by leading by example. Don't come home complaining about comments and concerns you received that day or week. Teach them how to let it go and move on.

REFLECTION:

1. Write down ways that you may be guilty of keeping your kid in a fish bowl.

2. How can you take steps toward letting them grow a bit while still under your roof?

KID-IPULATION

Josie's father was pastoring a smaller church. Her family had formed many bonds with several church members. They loved and cared for these people deeply. Josie is now a grown woman. She shared with me that one of the deacons that had grown so close to her family actually had molested her as a child. She was afraid to tell her parents. She was embarrassed and hurting and never told a soul until she was grown. Josie dealt with many issues in her life stemming from these painful memories. Had Josie just told her parents they would have taken action immediately. She stayed quiet and lived in shame. Josie, feeling like she couldn't share this with her parents, felt rejected and alone. How could her father love this man? How could her parents love him and treat him like family? How could they not see what he was doing? It took Josie many years but thankfully she walks with the Lord today and has received complete emotional healing. You see, this man earned the trust of her parents and for a few years he used that trust to hurt Josie.

Many PKs have shared stories of adults being close to their parents who treated them poorly. PK's have spoken of church members correcting them, yelling at them and even thumping them from time to time. PK's have heard from churchgoers that their hair was not combed, their skirt was too short or their choice of church clothes were dirty or inappropriate. A PK once shared, "Unbeknownst to my parents some members of the church felt it was their duty to make sure I was always on my best behavior. I was flicked, glared at and even popped on the head with a Frisbee once." As pastors you need to communicate not only to your kids but also with your congregation about boundaries with your family. Your family is yours and churchgoers do not need to be encouraged to advise or direct your children. I don't believe that there is anything wrong with people getting onto our children when they are acting inappropriately, or just plain being naughty. The bummer is that some people take this to the extreme and feel the need to make an example of the Pastors' kids. It is so important to use caution when establishing relationships with your church family. Your children need to know the distinct difference between what is healthy and what is not. As a parent your first and top calling should be raising your kids and carefully considering the people that you allow to speak into their lives.

Shelly, a grown pastor's kid, shared this story with me. "I'll never forget the time a lovely, well-meaning lady told me that I needed to leave my father alone on a Saturday so that he would not have to deal with any stress before church. This woman proceeded to say that my father (her pastor) was stressed out by all the grandkids and needed space to make sure he was having enough time to prepare his sermon. I was so hurt. I had been spending wonderful Saturdays bringing my family on a pretty lengthy road trip to spend weekends with my parents. We would spend entire afternoons playing baseball and just hanging out, in fact this time was really repairing a broken relationship between my parents and me. My parents were giving up their Saturdays to spend time with my family and enjoying every second. It really was a wonderful time for the whole family. This 'well-meaning' woman who attends the church in one sentence totally deflated me."

What in the world made this woman comfortable enough to approach a grown adult (Shelly) and let her know that she is a burden to her parents? Fact is that it just wasn't even the truth, but this woman felt it her duty to make sure Pastor Don would not be bothered on Saturdays so he could deliver the perfect message. There are so many things wrong with this story. One being that Shelly has struggled most of her life with feelings of rejection from her father. It took her years to build up a relationship with her dad that didn't make her feel as if she was a burden. She wondered if her father sent this woman so he wouldn't be the bad guy in the situation. It brought Shelly, a grown woman, back to the countless times she was asked to wait in the car or go to her room so that troubled people could have an audience with her parents. My own experience is the same, church members have told me to quiet down, sit still and take that lipstick off…all in hopes of impressing my parents or protecting them. In some twisted turn of events this churchgoer felt the need to stand up for her pastor knowing he was tired and needed rest. When someone was trying to be helpful to their pastor they did irreparable damage to his children.

Friends for Benefits

Sometimes kidipulation can totally go the opposite way. Some people will feel the desire to be close to you (their pastors) so they start with your children. They go out of their way to form a relationship with your child all the while hoping that you will take notice. This is not always the case of course but it happens more often than you may think. Daily I pray for God to bring positive mentors into my children's lives. However when I see a relationship forming with somebody that I don't feel like God has put in place for my kids, I really have no problem putting an end to it. I feel like a grown adult taking an over interest in my child is definitely something that we as parents really need to be aware of and watching for.

Some churchgoers feel the need to ask personal questions about your family and seek a personal relationship with your children in order to obtain information, for whatever reason. I personally have experienced this with not only myself but also my children. It's silly seemingly innocent questions that will give these certain people just enough of a glimpse into your lives to form an opinion or start a rumor. These questions vary but are usually like, "Does your mom keep your house clean?" "Do your parents argue a lot?" Or even, "Do you guys have beer in your fridge too?" It can be such a sad form of manipulation.

Not all parishioners do this, not all of them have ulterior motives. Most grown PK's agreed that in hindsight it was happening all along but when you are young and wanting attention you will take it from whoever will give it. I still struggle sometimes trying to understand people's need to be close to the pastor. PK's have written how they often wonder as grown adults why people try to compete with them for their parents' attention or worse, their love.

Jared, a Pastor's son, was sharing with me how there is a man in his church who is always around demanding his father's attention. He shared with me how it is hard to get a word in edgewise with this man around because he felt this man was always trying to compete with him. This man would even brag about the time he was spending with Jared's father. Deep down this PK was very jealous of the audience this man had with his father. Jared for years dealt with a jealousy issue that drove a wedge between him and his father. He felt like his role as a son had been taken from him and given to someone else. Jared has worked very hard to ignore this man and have a healthy relationship with his father, but the fact remains that this churchgoer is so dependant on the Pastor that Jared feels like his father has grown to enjoy being needed and has nurtured this unhealthy relationship unknowingly. To this day, there is a strained relationship between Jared and his father that is totally fixable and unnecessary. Understanding the need of this man to have the pastor's full attention is perplexing to me but so common among pastors and pastor's kids. There may be a person in your church right now or even another staff member that is requiring too much of your time and attention. Don't let people detour your relationship with your children. According to several PK's I've interviewed, this happens most of the time without your knowledge. Sometimes people can unknowingly hinder the development of your relationship with your kids just by saying a few thoughtless words, or demanding too much of your attention.

HELPFUL HINTS:

1. Guard your home. Many PK's have shared with me stories about people treating them badly in their own homes. Something that my husband and I have done in youth ministry with teenagers that come over is we tell them, "This is our kids' home and they share us with all of you so please respect them. If they are watching a show, don't change the channel. Ask them

before you use their things like games and videos.
Never disrespect them or boss them around. We are
the parents and we will deal with our children. No
joke cracking or belittling." It is so crazy the things
that people feel like they can tell your kids when
you're not around. The sad thing is that at certain ages
these comments can affect your child in very negative
ways and you may never know about it. Please never
let your kids feel like a stranger in their own homes.

2. Do not be afraid to ask your children how church
    members treat them when you are not around. Children
    are good at seeing things at face value. They can help
    you be able to see when people are being real or not.
    Let your church members know that you love them
    and you appreciate their concern for your family, but
    please direct the concerns to you. All children should be
    taught to respect authority, and as PK's they will need to
    learn how to smile, nod and move on. There is a place
    occasionally when we all need someone to ask the kids
    messing around in the back to be quite. It may be a good
    idea to set up in advanced with a family member or close
    friend to help keep an eye on your kids while you are
    ministering. Set expectations before service for behavior
    and discipline guidelines for the watcher and your kids.
    Please do not put someone in a situation that could be
    harmful to your kids or create an offense between you

and a parishioner. A clearly laid plan will help everyone see your kids as a priority even while you are behind a pulpit, microphone or a desk.

3. Draw the line about family. It may be in the best interest of your children to have a choice on whether or not to call every person over fifty grandma or grandpa. Remind your children of who your family is, re-enforce those relationships and ask your family to take time to pour into your kid's life. Their unconditional love is paramount. It is so important to use caution when establishing relationships with your church family. Your children need to know the distinct difference between what is real and what is not. The difference you will see when someone directs your kids with their best interests at heart will be worth the extra effort. We all want our kids to be the most well rounded, best-behaved cherubs in the world, but at the cost of long-term damage is it really worth it? We are only pastors for a season but we are parents for the rest of our lifetime. Some people like to use the term, "It takes a village to raise a child." I have nothing against a village raising a child if that village is just being a support structure for you and your wife/ husband. Please do not let your child become "The Village Idiot."

REFLECTION:

1. Do you have your family values posted in your home?

2. Do you clearly state rules of your home with frequent guests? Youth pastors, do your youth kids know the rules with your kids and in your home?

3. Make the rules of the home and post them now for people to see.

4. Is there a person in your church or maybe even a staff member that requires more of your time than others? Identify these people and begin to make your "exit strategy."

SPIRITUAL WAR-SCARE

As pastor's kids or kids raised in ministry, we are exposed to a lot of things that other kids wouldn't be exposed to. In the charismatic church this is more prevalent than some other denominations. Most small kids are shielded from scary movies, no parent would even dream of letting their children watch *Poltergeist* or the *Blair Witch Project.* That would just be too scary. All to often pastors kids have been exposed to the same type of talk and mental images. Some parents go as far as not letting their kids watch anything involving magic, I've heard lot's of PK's say their parents would not let them eat lucky charms, watch the Smurfs, and they had to refer to the, "Dirt Devil" as the "Dirt Angel."

I can't tell you the laughs some PK's had over this. Not because we had these rules but because so many of us shared almost the exact same memories. Most of the PK's I interviewed were thrilled that other people experienced these things. Parents go to great lengths to shield their kids from things entering their children's minds and hearts but sometimes completely overlook things that can be much more harmful. For instance, I can recall hearing people share openly with my parents about demons, Satan, angels, sprits, and the paranormal. Starting at a young age, we are told how to have faith, and with that faith, we can just say the name of Jesus and the devil has to leave.

Okay, so here I am in a dark room about nine years old, this morning I heard a woman sharing about casting a demon out of her son during prayer meeting. Unfortunately, I am so paralyzed with fear that I can't even mutter the name of Jesus. When I finally do get the courage to whisper His name, I know the devil has to leave. Does that mean that he has to leave my room, my house, or is he waiting outside my bedroom window? I vaguely remember a roaring lion seeking that he may devour. Great! There may be a Lion outside of my room and my parents are at the other end of the house. Another whisper "Jesus," hopefully that one will cause Satan to at least flee to my sister's room.

Children obviously deal better in the natural, with things that they can see. Unfortunately, when fear takes over kids can't see demons leaving, or Jesus coming to the rescue. A parent shared a story with me about her eight-year-old son being taught to cast demons out of people in Sunday school. Now don't get me wrong, battling the enemy is important to know how to do, but the presentation needs to be consistent with the audience. This particular child promptly shared his newfound knowledge with his younger brother. Being the authority on such deep spiritual things he certainly highlighted the way that demons can hide, harm and make life generally bad.

After several nights of crying and allowing her young sons to sleep with the light on she finally uncovered the truth. Her sons were afraid to sleep in their own room because they were convinced the curtains moving were demons moving around their room. Understanding her children's need for a parallel they could understand she turned to super heros. She took her children outside and drew a line all the way around her house. The line she explained represented the blood of Jesus and that his blood created a force field. We all know that a force field cannot be crossed by the bad guys. Her children have slept soundly since. I am not saying that we should always use movies or worldly things to explain God but I am saying we should use what works.

Another PK shared a story with me about spiritual warfare that still affects her today. "One night I was at a sleep over, and we fell asleep watching T.V. The next morning over breakfast we overheard my friend's mother explaining to my mom that as she walked into the room to shut the TV off, the program *Bewitched* was on and she could see little black demons jumping out of the T.V." Fast forward to present day and the reason for this story. This woman is grown and has children of her own. She was in her garage working out and a commercial for a new *Bewitched* movie came on. She broke into a cold sweat and ran out of the garage as fast as her legs would carry her. She had to convince her husband that nothing was wrong, she just needed him to go out and turn the T.V. off. You see her husband is not a believer and there was no way he would understand her fear of demon possession. She still doesn't like going into her garage and has now shut off the cable out there. Overhearing this mother's comments left a lasting impression on her.

The presentation needing to be consistent with the audience is such an important thing to practice while raising a PK. Letting our kids see and hear too much of the spiritual world can be damaging to them if they are not ready for it.

> We as parents go through so much trouble to monitor the programs our kids watch on TV, the movies that they watch and the music they listen to, but we openly discuss the things which in fact can be a source of fear.

Ignorance is not bliss and I am not in favor of pretending that none of it exists; I am simply in favor of waiting until they are ready. Give them parts that they can understand at the time. Highlighting the victory, showing our children that God is the winner. Pray, let the Father be your guide. If you aren't sure where the line is with your children, please error on the side of caution. Kids learn at different rates and will give you clues to let you know they are ready. Please don't allow them to focus on the negative. Children should be taught evil in smaller portion to good. Make sure your child firmly understands how much the Father loves and protects them before teaching them that the power they are given by the Holy Spirit can banish evil. Possibly take a different approach and teach your children all the good that the power of the Holy Spirit can do, encourage, heal, lift up. Once your PK's have mastered the love aspect of God's power they may be more ready to understand how to use love in spiritual warfare, after all perfect love casts out all fear. Teach love and then they will have nothing to fear.

Scared into Heaven

So I'm lying in bed fast asleep. I'm twelve years old. I hear a loud horn, it sounds like a trumpet. I sit up, heart pounding, sweat dripping down my forehead and shout, "Jesus, forgive me of my sins!" The words from Matthew 24 ringing in my head, *"He will send forth his angels with the sound of a mighty trumpet blast, and they will gather together his chosen ones from the farthest ends of the earth and heaven…"* Did he come back? Did I miss the rapture? There it is again I have another chance, "Jesus forgive me of my sins!" I take a few seconds to gather myself, when I hear the sound one last time, HONK, HONK, HONNNNNNK. Finally realizing what the sound is I lay back down hoping nobody heard me mistaking a train coming through town for the rapture.

Sounds funny now, but it wasn't then. The worst part about this story is that every pastor's kid that I've spoken with has a similar story to tell. A PK from Montana tells a story of the time she came home from school and no one was there. So she started calling all of the elders of the church to see if the rapture had happened. Or the PK that watched a movie about the rapture and slept on the couch for a year after wards because she felt if she was close enough to her parents and the rapture happened, she could catch them and hold on to them. Another person from TN shared with me that she was afraid to go to bed without asking Jesus to forgive her of her sins in case He came back while she was asleep. She was worried that if she may have committed a sin without knowing it she could be left behind.

We have all read books and seen powerful movies that help make us resolute in our decision to follow a God we love, and encourage others to make a life decision for our savior. Media and conversation can be a powerful tool for our cause, a way to help us in our efforts to show people the light. For instance, the *Left Behind* series or the infamous *Thief in the Night* movie. As parents we need to educate our kids on all of these things but we may be wise to wait until they can understand. I don't know very many children who know Einstein's Theory of Relativity or Geometry. I don't know of many parents that have tried to share with their children how a light bulb works. It's just important that they know how to access the switch and that the switch serves a purpose, to illuminate. With things of a spiritual nature, it's ok for our kids to understand the purpose but not exactly how it works; speak in a way that you know your children will hear.

> Our most powerful moments of ministry come when we are with our children.

If these details of spiritual warfare or the end times cause anxiety then you aren't really leading your children, you may be demanding understanding. Never in scripture does God demand for us to understand, he is a non-anxious, influencing presence that leads us to understanding. God keeps us safe, He loves us and He will always be here to help us. It is disappointing to think that our children sometimes have an unhealthy fear of God. A fear that is not born out of respect and adoration but fear that is born out of misinformation and over teaching.

The grace of God is a beautiful thing, it propels us gently to greatness and a deeper sincerity. As parents we need that grace to get through some days. As a spouse we need it to get through most days and as a pastor we need it to get through every day. In teaching our kids about the grace of God we can also teach them that we are human, that we struggle to be good parents, spouses and leaders. Without getting scary spiritual we need to uncover spiritual truths that will help chart a course for greatness in our children. Understanding that the spirit of God is a beautiful thing not to live in fear of but to revel in. With the name of Jesus does come so much power. The power to show love or the power to create fear. I hope that we all take the time to teach our children that there truly is no sweeter name than the name of Jesus and yes it can make even the darkest hour fill with light.

HELPFUL HINTS:

1. Be in tune with your child. Always try to be gauging where they are spiritually and emotionally. Moms, you are the eyes and ears of the home for the most part. Communication between spouses is imperative. Be on the same page as to what you are teaching the children. We don't want Mom telling the kids, "The devil is a sly old fox." Then Dad telling the kids, "The devil is a roaring lion seeking to devour you." That may be a silly example but parents sending different messages is confusing. Talk with your spouse about how you will approach important issues in advance.

2. Make sure the presentation is consistent with the audience. Don't feel like you need to rush into telling your kids all about Revelation, the end times, and all the demonic activity going on in the world today. Teaching your children about these topics when they are ready and can understand will eliminate confusion. It will detour them from being a Christ

follower because they are fearful of what will happen to them if they do not serve the Lord. Your children's walk with God should always be motivated by love.

3. Don't compare your kids to other kids. Just because somebody else's kid has a deeper walk with Christ and has a firm understanding of the spiritual realm doesn't mean your child needs to. Every kid is different and some catch on faster. Don't pressure them to feel, speak, or understand more than they can comprehend.

REFLECTION:

1. Are your kids at an age where they can fully understand spiritual warfare, the end times, or things of this nature? (Remember the age may differ for each child)

2. Have you over shared with them or have they overheard you sharing with people about these things?

3. What can you do to teach your kids the truth without scaring them or possibly making them choose to follow Christ because they are fearful?

UDENTITY

"Hello, I'm _____. Pastor John's kid." We are all guilty of this, even some of us Pastors' wives. So for most of my life I introduced myself as Pastor Jim's kid, and people still refer to my husband and I like that sometimes. It felt good for me as a kid to go to church events and some camps and get special treatment cause I was Jim's kid. So you had better believe that everywhere I went, I made sure people knew that I was Pastor Jim's kid. Now fast forward a few years and imagine my surprise when I head off to Bible college. "Hi, I'm Re'na, Pastor Jim's kid." My director replied with, "Oh, who is Pastor Jim, where does he Pastor at?"

As I began to explain my father and all the amazing things he did for his community, how selfless and inspirational he was, my director just sat waiting for me to finish so we could move on in our studies. I felt sort of lost for a while. It used to be that I didn't have to work so hard for things in the church, so this was all new and different to me. I carried my identity through my dad for so long that I did not actually have a strong identity of my own.

A twenty-three-year-old PK in an interview once told me that she moved to a new city with her mother who was a children's pastor. She is grown and married and she just followed her parents to a new city. Her mother had been pastoring her whole life. So in this new city they found a church to attend and really liked it. She told me how she felt so weird there, almost like an outcast. She could recall the day she said to her mother, "Mom, you should apply for the open position here, nobody knows who we are." She had always found an identity with her mother's position and not who she was. It was hard for her to attend church without being a PK. She did not feel any worth without people knowing who she was.

So many PK's have used their father's position as leverage to get them ahead in life. Here is the problem with that, when we leave the house we are unsure how to be successful with out our dad's name behind us. It seems strange I know, but it is so real and also really hard to deal with. Another PK from Colorado once said that she always found her identity in her parents. Until the day that her father, who was the pastor of a pretty decent sized church, decided that he would have an affair with the church secretary. Still being in high school she was left not only bewildered by what had happened with her father but she felt like she had completely lost her identity. Going to church suddenly became very shameful. What was happening to her was the church people that she knew and loved and had become part of her family were suddenly shunning her. All of a sudden it was not just that her beloved father was a liar and a cheater but also some of the people who she loved most were acting awkward and uncomfortable around her and her mother. She felt so abandoned by just about everyone she knew. She realized for the first time in her life that she did not want to known as, Pastor Bill's kid any more. One day she was using his position to get special treatment the next day she was hanging her head in shame hoping people wouldn't notice her. Not only did she have to deal with the breaking apart of her family, she also had to deal with the falling apart of her church and relationships she had always held so dear.

Parents, it is so important that your kids know who they are. That they are proud to be your kids but that they should not use it to their advantage. Try your best to reiterate that they have the same privileges as any other kid in the church. My father chose the opposite route when we got a little older, my husband and I actually went to work for him in Montana. My dad had very high expectations on us and didn't let a lot slip because he didn't want anyone to think he was playing favorites. I really appreciate this for the most part. We had to earn the respect of the church and its people. It was a great experience to know that the people loved me for who I was and God's calling in my life and not for being the PK. I'm sure that there is a perfect balance in this area and I'm not going to lie to you, I haven't found it yet, but I'll do my best to be sure my kids do not leave the house feeling lost because they have to rebuild their confidence based upon their own talents and abilities. That's were we want it to be built in the first place. If we build our children independently, aside from our calling and allow for them to grow, on their own, I have no doubts that they will grow towards Jesus. It is difficult for a flower to bloom in the shade, ask yourself, is my pastoral calling casting the shadow?

God Has No Grandkids

Another aspect of udentity is your kids' belief system. Ok so your kids know their books of the Bible and more scripture than any other kids in the church and quite possibly the universe. PK's joke about knowing one hundred Bible verses but not knowing any nursery rhymes.

> Do your kids know why they believe what they believe? Or do they just believe because it is all they know?

PKs can quote tons of scripture but sometimes have no clue what it means.

I heard another PK once say that he knows scripture that he's never even read. The same PK also shared that some inspirational quotes he heard so often in his life, he didn't even know they were in the Bible. Imagine his surprise when he stumbled upon some of his favorite quotes while reading the

Bible. When your kids leave the house and begin to question what they believe, which will happen for sure, without you there as their backbone what do they have to stand on?

A PK in Nashville went through a really rough church split. During this split people left the church because some hubbub about the Holy Spirit. When asked her stance, all she knew was what she had been told by her parents. She had to do some real soul searching and studying to see why she believed these things. It was so strange to her when she realized that all she knew was not even biblical. When she finally called her mom and dad to ask what they thought she realized that her whole life what they taught her she completely misunderstood, leaving her to question her faith from all aspects.

Sometimes being a PK means that you forget about personal goals. Sometimes goals in life are all wrapped up in the church. Sometimes goals become about the size of the church, the success of their parents, but not about their own personal growth. PK's need to know that their personal walk with God is their number one priority. Because of personal experience I ask myself frequently,

"If I walked away from God tomorrow, would my kids still serve the Lord?"

The first time I talked this over with my husband I could hardly sleep. The thought of my own children not serving the

Lord almost makes me sick. My husband and I began a new approach with our children. In our times together we began to question their love for God. We started to tell them that they do not have to love Jesus or even go to church if they don't want to. All the while feeling sick that they may not choose to follow Him. We take a certain amount of risk doing this but I've interviewed too many PK's who do not serve the Lord and are quite bitter at the church. A PK friend of mine from Colorado shared with me that her father always told her, "God has no grandkids; you are either His child or you are not." Wow what a statement, it hit me like a ton of bricks.

> My children are not going to heaven to spend eternity with Jesus just because I am.

Sometimes as Pastors we assume that our kids are following Christ and living rightly related to Him; however, do we really know our kids' hearts? Do Pastors give their children the option to not serve God? Recently a PK who is now a successful pastor spoke of having a great experience growing up a PK. He speaks highly of his parents and has fond memories of childhood but also admits that he truly began to follow Christ in his late twenties when in college. I too began to serve the Lord on a personal level later in life. How can we as parents impress upon our children the importance of having a deep committed relationship with Jesus but also openly give them the choice? This sent me on a mission; I began to interview not just pastor's kids but also their parents. Some of these parents who have done a phenomenal job at raising well-adjusted kids who love Jesus. As every child is different and there is no one answer to this question. Having a solid foundation in God's Word is so important for our kids, but if they are learning it and not understanding it then we have a problem. Here few tips I picked up from Pastors who have raised children that still have a solid walk with the Lord.

HELPFUL HINTS:

1. The best advice I found is that just like everything else in life you have to lead by example. If you can lead an entire congregation you must be able to lead your family. Let your children see you and your husband/wife spending time with Jesus daily. One of my favorite speakers shared a message about spending time with the Father recently.

> *12 It was [a]at this time that He went off to the mountain to pray, and He spent the whole night in prayer to God. Luke 6:12(NIV)*

He shared about when Jesus went on the mountain to pray. If Jesus had to go away to spend time with the Father, then how much *more* time do we need to spend with Him? I found that so invaluable in my walk with Jesus. Having a steady quiet time is monumental for you but it is equally important for your kids to witness. Let them see the importance of this time and share with them often how crucial it is. Always lead by example.

2. Challenge your kids. By this I mean, when they give you the standard answers that you want to hear, or that they have been trained to say, for example, You ask, "Why do we love Jesus?" and your kids answer with the standard PK answer, "Because he gave his life for us, he died and took our sins away," etc. You know what I mean. DIG DEEPER. Ask questions like, Why does that even matter? Why do you love Him? You don't have to love him you know. When you dig a little deeper they have to think a little harder. Those PK pre-written answers won't work. When your children have a stance on something really poke around to make sure they not only know what they are talking about, but also that they feel conviction about it.

3. Pray. Spend time praying for your children. Spend time in prayer with your children, not just before meals and bed. Spend time praying for lost friends, school teachers, and missionaries. Make prayer a staple in your life, teaching your kids that we pray any time of day for all different situations. Showing them the power of prayer and how much we rely on God is

so important. We want our children growing up with the habit of always talking to the Lord and bringing everything to Him in prayer and thanksgiving.

4. If your kids are not asking you questions about God, Jesus, The Holy Spirit and other things of that nature then they may just be uninterested. This can good indicator of where they are spiritually. Bring up having Faith in God whenever possible. If they are not asking you questions, then make sure to ask them questions.

REFLECTION:

1. Think of a list of questions you can ask your kids that can help you gauge where they are spiritually. Really pry to see how firm their foundation is.

2. Make a prayer list with your kids. Ask them who they want to pray for. Pray over the list as a family and challenge your kids to pray on their own. Always come back to recognize answers to prayers and praise the Lord together.

3. Do your kids ask questions about their faith. Do they seem interested or indifferent?

THE CATAPULT TO EXPLORATION

I can recall sitting in a room with some of my sister's friends talking about boys one night. I was so excited that she didn't kick me out of her room although she should have. They were all much older than me and definitely not on the same path of life that I was on. I remember one girl who wasn't a Jesus follower would openly share of her sexual experiences with boys. Like most young girls these conversations piqued my interest in all things boy related. Of the surveys I took, 9 out of 10 of the PK's had had sex before they were married. Six out of those were with more than one partner. Astounding right? This is so devastating to parents when they find out. PK's explained to me that their parents believed that:

1. Their kids will make the right choices because of the way that they were raised.

2. Or that their kids won't even be approached by these things because of who they are.

This way of thinking makes things easier on parents. Unfortunately according to teenage boys, pastors' daughters have quite the reputation. Even my husband openly admits that a lot of boys were after the pastor's daughters due to this stigma. If you think that your kids will automatically know what to do in a situation where they are getting too close to their boyfriend or girlfriend you are sadly mistaken, no matter how many times you have lectured them, or given them the talk; your kids are going to be excited and curious just like any other teenager. Parents, not talking to your kids about this is the very worst thing you can do to them.

A PK once told me that he actually learned about masturbation from his older sister's boyfriend. Some learned from their friends at school. Having the mindset that if we shield our kids from the world we can keep them from experiencing or being approached by things of sexual nature is dangerous. Working with teenagers I am completely shocked by how early they are talking about sex and actually experimenting with it. I have students as early at the sixth grade that have lost their virginity. I have sixth grade girls that have kissed other girls because the boys think that it's cool. I have worked with PK's and visited with young PK's who felt like their parents had no idea what they were going through when it came to dating and relationships. I've encountered this personally with my thirteen-year-old.

Taking my own advice and the advice of other PK's in this area I've found to be actually quite challenging. Luckily my husband has been having most of the birds and the bees talks with our son. However the things he is hearing at school are mind blowing to me. Having to explain things to my son that I didn't find out about till I was much, much older has been very hard. So many PK's have expressed that they only wished they could feel comfortable enough to talk to their parents about these things. In light of all my conversations with PK's my husband and I have really placed a high priority on being the ones to have the awkward conversations with our kids. I will admit although totally uncomfortable at times, it is so beneficial for us and our kids. Finding out later in life that it is much harder to undo confused ideas about puberty, sex, and relationships than it is to just lay it all out there ourselves.

I recently had the opportunity to personally experience the birds and bees talk. My son came home from school with all kinds of questions about a web site he heard about at school. My first reaction was to run and hide hoping that he would forget about it. As my husband and I discussed our next course of action my husband felt like it was his duty to have the talk with our boy, and I was completely in agreement. Now I should have just let that be the end of it but just like any other mother, I sat quietly outside the door and was amazed at the honesty and love that my husband showed my son. They had a few laughs and awkward silences from time to time but it was a very successful conversation. Literally no question was left unanswered and even questions my son didn't want to ask got answered. This conversation did so many things for our family and really made my son feel comfortable talking to us about really difficult issues.

A handful of PK's have shared stories with me about it being pure torture talking to their parents about things involving sex, puberty, and anything related, letting me know that they were mostly painful because their parents were uncomfortable. As I dug deeper I began to realize several issues with parents' lack of conversations with their kids. Some PK's are informed but completely in a backward way. These PK's have grown up hearing all the bad things about sex. They have heard countless stories, sermons, lectures, and gossip about people who have committed sexual sins or had negative experiences when it comes to sex. Parents have inadvertently given the impression that sex is wrong, dirty, disgusting and immoral. How many times have you talked to your children about the dangers of pre-marital sex and all that goes along with that? We don't hesitate to paint a picture to our teenagers of the filthy, immoral side of sex, but we rarely counter that sentiment with the beauty of God creating man and woman and that He created sex for and man and his wife. How often do we sit our kids down and say, "Hey sex is awesome, it is a beautiful thing that God created for us to enjoy"? How many times have you said anything positive about sex at all to your children? Now I'm not saying we should talk about it all the time and give details or personal accounts. Let's not gross them out.

A wonderful mother who serves at church recently shared with me how she imparts to her kids that sex is awesome, it's from the Lord and can be so wonderful but ONLY and I mean ONLY in the context of marriage. She shared with me the balance of teaching your children about sex in both lights, the good and the bad. Not always driving home the negative parts. It can be very awkward to share this with your children but at the same time they are going to find out eventually that you and your husband/wife do have sex. (Well at least once, and that was to conceive right?)

While interviewing a PK who had just been married a few months she spoke with me about her struggles with intimacy. She really made me realize just how important it is to educating our kids about sex properly. This PK shared with me that when she was first married to her husband she really struggled with intimacy. She felt for a few months that being intimate with her husband didn't seem right. It still seemed a little dirty or sinful. She grew up learning of all the dangers and negative things that come along with sex and was able to abstain from sex until marriage. Her lack of knowledge and preparedness from her parents limited her growth in an intimate relationship with her husband. She shared with me that if she had been educated even just a little things would have been better. She had to overcome some big hurdles in the beginning of her marriage because she was completely uninformed, nervous, and had only ever heard that sex is wrong. I completely understood this, realizing that I, at times, am guilty of only speaking of sex in a bad light to my children. Because of years of working with teenagers and seeing the effects of pre-marital sex I have almost made my kids fearful of it. At this point in time I admit that it wouldn't bother me to keep them thinking it's of the devil, however long term effects are not worth the temporary relief of me knowing that they might make good choices in dating relationships. I cannot stress to you the importance of being open and honest with your kids about these issues. It is likely to be brutally awkward most of the time but completely necessary.

> Too many PK's explained their first encounters with the opposite sex as very unhealthy. Many of them explained that their lack of knowledge was a catapult to exploration.

With this generation having sex thrown at them from all directions, e.g. commercials, TV, billboards, magazines, peers, and the internet, if we aren't the ones explaining sex, relationships, masturbation, etc., with them don't worry about it because it is right at their fingertips and being hurled at them on a daily basis. Unhealthy worldviews of sex, relationships and dating are being taught to them constantly. Subtle hints about sexuality are even dropped into popular kids T.V. shows, making our kids believe that it is ok to disobey their parents, date, kiss, make out and other things all without their parents even knowing.

Every child will encounter a time in their lives where they are really curious about their body and all things to do with their body. What you do during this time can shape how they approach sex and dating but can also shape parts of their marriage. Being honest is critical; I've personally made the mistake of thinking that my children were in the dark about sex and other issues. I thought that they were too young and not ready to have the talk. My husband and I knew we needed to sit down with our son soon and discuss these matters, but unfortunately a young man at the lunch table took it upon himself to educate my son on porn and other issues. My husband later had to explain in great detail that this young man was wrong not only in what he was saying but also wrong to be speaking like that in public. Parents, it's naive to think that you can shield your kids from these things happening. I now have gotten a jump-start with my daughter after hearing that she knew what sex was from some kids on the playground. Although she wasn't entirely accurate, she was close enough for me to be concerned. I have to admit, being honest with her is at times very uncomfortable. But I desperately want my children to have a healthy view on sex and relationships and not a worldly view.

HELPFUL HINTS:

1. Never assume that your kids don't know about sex or sexual things. All kids are different and their development differs, but their exposure to it is happening more than you may think. In doing research for this chapter the statistics I read were staggering

and a bit scary to be honest. Kids are getting involved in sexual activity at younger ages every year.

2. Having, "the talk" is never a one-time thing. Keep the lines of communication open always. The sex talk should be reoccurring while your kids are growing up and being exposed to more and more. Be honest and up front, always leaving room for more and more questions.

3. Be prepared in advance with topics you need to cover with your kids. If you know what you are going to say in advance you can give the best information possible without fumbling or making it even more awkward. A good offense is the best defense.

4. Do research. Look up ideas on how to approach your kids, maybe some ideas on questions to ask, etc. With a little research you can get ideas on what kids are dealing with today as opposed to what we as parents encountered. Focus on the Family has some great info in dealing with your kids and sex, pornography and other things of this nature.

5. Speak with them privately. Let them know how important it is to you and to their future. Set aside some time and be prepared to answer all of their questions.

6. Use medical terms while talking about sex. Penis, vagina, breasts, etc. Using other terms can make it seem less important and sometimes silly. Making sure that these talks are taken seriously is of utmost importance.

7. Frequently ask your kids questions, giving them an opportunity to share with you things that you may not know. Examples of this could be, "Is there anything you would like to share with us today?" "How do you feel about _____?" What is your perspective on sex, dating, relationships, etc.? Give them a chance to share with you so you can know if you are getting through to them or not.

8. Let them know sex is a gift from God. Always follow up talks with how God designed sex to be for a man and wife. Never talk about it in a shaming or condemning way. Always speaking of sex in a negative way can cause damage in the future.

9. If you haven't done it yet, go check your computers and electronic devices around your house. This is especially important if your kids are pre-teen and teens. Check your internet history for anything suspicious. If the history is deleted, than you have a problem and need to confront your child.

REFLECTION:

1. Have you had, "the talk"? If not take a few moments and write down your game plan. Things you need to cover.

2. Write 5 questions you can ask your son/ daughter about sex and relationships. Let them write 5 questions for you to answer honestly for them.

YOU MIGHT BE A PASTOR'S KID IF...

- If you have ever hidden secular music under your mattress, you might be a PK.

- If you go to a church lock in, and you don't have to pack an overnight bag.

- If you know 50 bible verses before you know any nursery rhymes.

- If you know the books of the Bible better than the alphabet.

- If you feel guilt even thinking about sinning.

- If you go to the nursing home on a regular basis and you don't know anyone there.

- If you call a bunch of people with absolutely no relation to you brother, sister, grandma, grandpa, ect.

- If you attend men's Bible study, women's Bible study, golden heirs study, celebrate recovery, and divorce care all in one week.

- If you attend men's Bible study, women's Bible study, golden heirs study, celebrate recovery, and divorce care but you are only 7.

- If your parents quote Colossians 3:20 to you all the time.

- If you're at church as much as you are at home.

- If your life mistakes are used to help people.

- If your most embarrassing moments are shared from the platform.

- If you were not allowed to watch anything involving magic but your parents talk openly about Satan and demons and you have seen possessed people prayed over.

- If you have ever played, "underneath the sheets" with the hymnal on Sunday morning.

- If your car breaks down and your only mode of transportation is a 15-passenger van.

- If you are the only adult in the nursery and you're 12.

- If you have ever worn a coffee ground beard, towel on your head and a bathrobe for Halloween.

- If you've only been to church harvest parties for Halloween.

- If while your friends were pretending to be in a rock band, you and your siblings were playing worship team.

- If you are afraid to go to sleep without asking Jesus to forgive you of your sins, just in case the rapture happens while you are sleeping.

- If you have had the lead role in every church play you have ever been in.

- If the only professional athlete you know is Tim Tebow.

- If you can name 20 big name pastors but not 20 celebrities.

- If you've ever gone school clothes shopping at a Christian book store.

- If you weren't allowed to say, "Pot Luck" you had to say "Pot blessing."

- If your Saturday morning cartoons included Bible man.

- If you've confused Bible stories with the Veggie Tales version.

- If all your dishes, cake pans and serving bowls have your last name written on the bottom.

- If you can't make it to the kitchen because your dad is counseling someone in the living room.

- If you have to rush home after church to clean because someone has invited themselves over for lunch.

- If you spend every Saturday in Nov/Dec practicing for the Christmas play.

- If you live close enough to the church to use its WI-FI.

- If you volunteer to set up and serve at pot lucks so you can see who brings what and know what is safe to eat or not. (You never know what kind of meat certain people put in their casseroles)

- If you do a bible quiz challenge and everyone wants you on their team.

- If you've ever done your hair and make up in a church bathroom.

- If you show up to church and hour early and you feel late.

- If you've ever brought your homework to church because you know you are going to be there all day.

- If you've sang at a wedding but had no idea who the bride and groom were.

Growing up a PK has its setbacks but can also be an incredible blessing. How that looks for your children is completely up to you.

You are building the kingdom from behind that pulpit but also from the high school bleachers and the preschool play mat, your family is part of the kingdom and your greatest mission. Have grace, that beautiful, strong family of yours will mess up, you will mess up and your kids, it's guaranteed that they will mess up. Apply grace liberally, add some laughter and maybe a few tears. It's okay to be broken and sorry to your children, as long as you have a plan for restoration, your weakness with show them strength.

My prayer for you is that this book has brought you a new awareness in some way. I hope that you will take what you have read and put it into action. Even if it is just one thing.